Emily's Christmas Gifts

Emily Post

Emily's Christmas Gifts

by CINDY POST SENNING, Ed.D., and PEGGY POST
illustrated by STEVE BJÖRKMAN

Collins
An Imprint of HarperCollinsPublishers

We dedicate this book to our parents, Betty and Ferd and Libby and Bill, with love and deep
appreciation for *so* many happy Christmases.
—P.P. and C.P.S.

For Jo Skibby, who knows and loves kids
—S.B.

Emily Post is a registered trademark of The Emily Post Institute, Inc.

Collins is an imprint of HarperCollins Publishers.
Emily's Christmas Gifts
Text copyright © 2008 by The Emily Post Institute, Inc.
Illustrations copyright © 2008 by Steve Björkman
Manufactured in China.

Library of Congress Cataloging-in-Publication Data
Senning, Cindy Post.
    Emily's Christmas gifts / by Cindy Post Senning, Ed.D., and Peggy Post ; illustrated by Steve Björkman. —
1st ed.
        p. cm.
    Summary: In the sometimes hectic days before Christmas, Emily's family appreciates her gifts of caring,
sharing, helping, smiling, and loving. Includes a note for parents on how to encourage good manners during
the holiday season.
    ISBN 978-0-06-111703-9 (tr bdg.) — ISBN 978-0-06-111704-6 (lb bdg.)
    [1. Christmas—Fiction. 2. Gifts—Fiction. 3. Conduct of life—Fiction. 4. Etiquette—Fiction. 5. Family
life—Fiction.] I. Post, Peggy, 1945- II. Björkman, Steve, ill. III. Title.
PZ7.S476Em 2008   2007027228
[E]—dc22   CIP
                                                                                                   AC

Typography by Jeanne L. Hogle
1 2 3 4 5 6 7 8 9 10
❖
First Edition

No one loves Christmas
more than Emily.

She loves everything about the holiday:

the carols,

the food,

the decorations,

and the gifts.

When she was little, all Emily could think about was getting presents.

Now that she is a big girl, she loves giving gifts, too.

Some gifts Emily wraps up in pretty packages to be opened on Christmas morning. But the most special gifts she gives won't go under the tree.

These are the gifts of kindness and consideration. Even though they don't cost a cent, everyone appreciates them.

Mom is so thankful when Emily gives her help
setting the table and making special place cards
for Christmas dinner.

Dad is thrilled when Emily gives him a hand putting up the Christmas lights.

Grandpa and Grandma
are overjoyed to receive big
welcoming hugs and help
with their coats and bags,

while Nutmeg loves that Emily gives him
an afternoon playing in the snow.

These gifts are not just for friends and family. They are for everyone. Emily gives a small kindness here,

and a little consideration there.

Everyone is so busy during the holidays. There is so much to do before Christmas Day:

the shopping,

the cleaning,

and the cooking.

It's no wonder that sometimes people can feel tired and a little cranky.

Emily's special gifts are
exactly what everyone
wants and needs most.

Even Emily! You see, she's not the only one who knows about giving special gifts. She knows because she gets them, too.

On Christmas Eve everything is ready:
The stockings are hung,
the tree is trimmed,
and the presents are wrapped.

But wait! Emily has one more gift and a special
thank-you to give someone . . .

Emily

Dear Santa,
I wanted to tell you that Christmas is
my favorite holiday and thank you for the
great gifts.
Love,
Emily P.

P.S. I made these tuna fish sandwiches for you.
I thought they might make a nice change
from cookies.

P.P.S. The carrots are for your reindeer.

. . . someone who loves to give gifts as much as Emily does.

Emily

Naughty   Nice

☐ Mean   ☑ Kind
☑ Impatient   ☐ Patient
☐ Messy   ☑ Neat
☐ Rude   ☑ Polite
☐ Sneaky   ☑ Honest
☐ Greedy   ☑ Genee

Santa Claus

Dear Emily,
You are most welcome for the gifts. Thank you for the tuna fish. It was just what I wanted for Christmas.

Love,
Santa

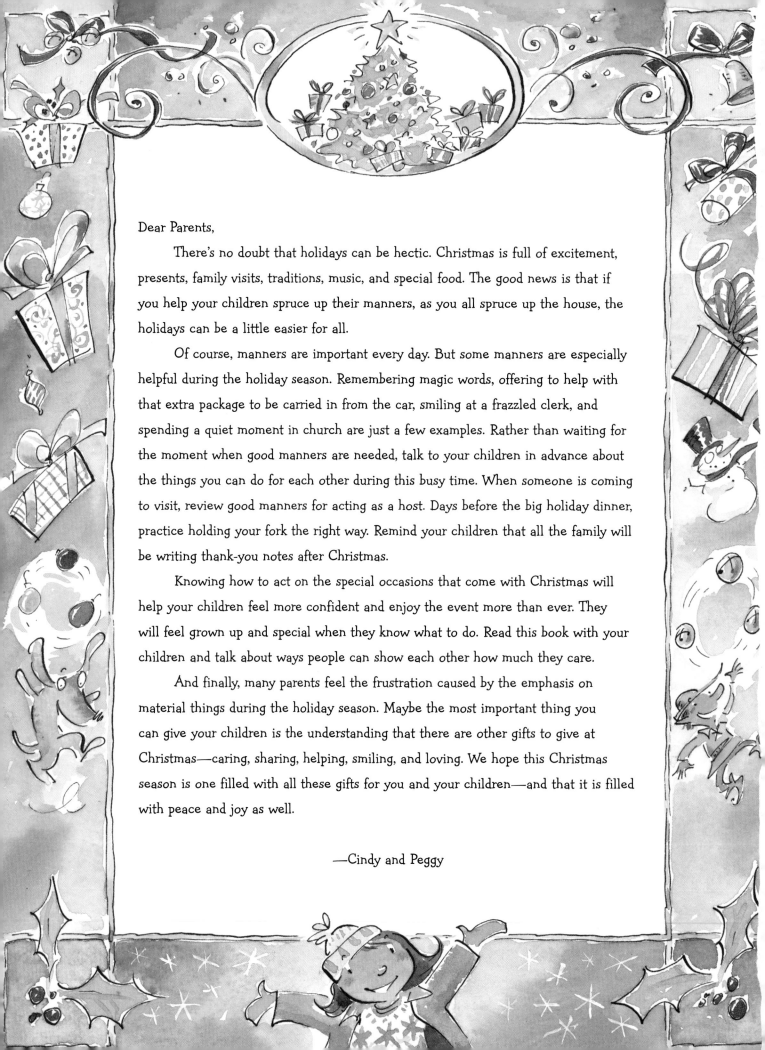

Dear Parents,

There's no doubt that holidays can be hectic. Christmas is full of excitement, presents, family visits, traditions, music, and special food. The good news is that if you help your children spruce up their manners, as you all spruce up the house, the holidays can be a little easier for all.

Of course, manners are important every day. But some manners are especially helpful during the holiday season. Remembering magic words, offering to help with that extra package to be carried in from the car, smiling at a frazzled clerk, and spending a quiet moment in church are just a few examples. Rather than waiting for the moment when good manners are needed, talk to your children in advance about the things you can do for each other during this busy time. When someone is coming to visit, review good manners for acting as a host. Days before the big holiday dinner, practice holding your fork the right way. Remind your children that all the family will be writing thank-you notes after Christmas.

Knowing how to act on the special occasions that come with Christmas will help your children feel more confident and enjoy the event more than ever. They will feel grown up and special when they know what to do. Read this book with your children and talk about ways people can show each other how much they care.

And finally, many parents feel the frustration caused by the emphasis on material things during the holiday season. Maybe the most important thing you can give your children is the understanding that there are other gifts to give at Christmas—caring, sharing, helping, smiling, and loving. We hope this Christmas season is one filled with all these gifts for you and your children—and that it is filled with peace and joy as well.

—Cindy and Peggy